A Comprehensive Guide to Pi Coin Network and Blockchain Technology

Unlocking the Future: What You Need to Know About the Groundbreaking Smartphone-Based Cryptocurrency Mining for Beginners & Experts

Joel B. Albert

ALL RIGHTS RESERVED

No part of this book may be reproduced, distributed, or transmitted in any form or by any means, including photocopying, recording, or other electronic or mechanical methods, without the prior written permission of the author, except in the case of brief quotations embodied in critical reviews and certain other noncommercial uses permitted by copyright law. Unauthorized use of any content from this book is strictly prohibited and may result in legal action. For permission requests, write to the author or publisher.

Copyright © 2024, Jeol B. Albert

DISCLAIMER

The information provided in this book is intended for educational and informational purposes only. It is not financial, investment, legal, or professional advice. The views and opinions expressed in this book are those of the author and do not necessarily reflect the official policy or position of Pi Network or any associated entities.

The reader is encouraged to conduct their own research and consult with a qualified professional before making any financial decisions related to PiCoin, Pi Network, or blockchain technology.

The author and publisher disclaim any liability for any financial losses or damages that may arise from the use or reliance on the content of this book.

One Of Our Recent Books On Amazon

The Complete Bitcoin Exchange Traded Funds Handbook

TABLE OF CONTENTS

Introduction
Chapter 1
Overview Of Cryptocurrency
- The Evolution of Money
- Understanding Digital Assets

Chapter 2
The Rise of Pi Network
- The Vision Behind Pi Network
- The Founders and Their Mission

Chapter 3
How Pi Cryptocurrency Works
- The Pi Mining Process
- Pi's Consensus Algorithm

Chapter 4
Blockchain Technology Simplified
- What is Blockchain?
- How Pi's Blockchain Differs

Chapter 5
Getting Started with Pi Network
- Setting Up Your Pi Account (A Step-by-Step Guide)
- Building Your Pi Network (Referrals and Security Circles)

Chapter 6
The Pi Ecosystem
- Pi as a Medium of Exchange (Potential Use Cases)

    Developing Decentralized Applications(DApps)
Chapter 7
Believers vs. Skeptics Perspectives on Pi
    The Optimistic View and Why Pi Could Succeed
    The Critical View, Skepticism, and Concerns
Chapter 8
Pi Network in the Global Cryptocurrency Landscape
    How Pi Compares to Established Cryptocurrencies
    The Role of Pi in Developing Economies
Chapter 9
The Path to Pi's Mainnet
    From Testnet to Mainnet
    What to Expect When Pi Goes Live
Chapter 10
The Future of Pi and Cryptocurrency
    Predicting Pi's Impact on the Global Economy
    What Comes After Pi?
    Pi Network White Paper
CONCLUSION

INTRODUCTION

A Journey Toward Financial Freedom!
As the world stands on the cusp of a new financial revolution, many find themselves grappling with the complexities and uncertainties of the digital age. In an era where traditional banking systems and financial instruments are being challenged by the rise of cryptocurrencies, the need for clear, accessible guidance has never been more pressing.

This book is not just another technical manual or a speculative guide to getting rich quick; it is a treasure for those seeking to understand and harness the potential of a groundbreaking new cryptocurrency—Pi Coin.

And who better to guide you on this journey than Joel B. Albert, a passionate financial coach, monetary investment educator, and cryptocurrency enthusiast whose mission is to empower individuals of all ages with the knowledge and skills to achieve financial freedom.

Joel B. Albert's dedication to financial literacy is deeply rooted in his belief that everyone, regardless of their background or prior knowledge, should have the opportunity to participate in and benefit from the evolving financial landscape. With a wealth of expertise in finance and a talent for simplifying complex concepts, Joel has spent years helping people navigate the often intimidating world of money management.

His approach is unique, blending practical financial advice with a deep understanding of the digital money ecosystem. Through his coaching, teaching, and writing, Joel has touched the lives of countless individuals, guiding them toward making informed investment decisions, unlocking their financial potential, and building lasting wealth.

The Changing Face of Finance!

To appreciate the significance of Pi Coin and the broader world of cryptocurrencies, it is essential to understand the context in which they have emerged. Over the past few decades, the financial landscape has undergone a profound transformation. The advent of the internet, the globalization of markets, and the rise of digital technology have all contributed to a shift in how we think about and manage money. Traditional banking systems, once the bedrock of global finance, are now being supplemented—and in some cases, challenged—by a new breed of digital assets.

Cryptocurrencies, the most well-known of which is Bitcoin, have captured the imagination of millions. These digital currencies promise a world where financial transactions are faster, cheaper, and more secure, free from the control of centralized authorities.

However, as with any emerging technology, cryptocurrencies have also sparked debate and controversy. For every person who sees them as the future of money, there is another who views them with skepticism or fear. This dichotomy is at the heart of the challenge faced by anyone seeking to understand and engage with digital currencies.

Amid the noise and confusion, Pi Coin emerges as a distinctive and promising new player in the cryptocurrency space.
Pi Coin's mission aligns perfectly with Joel B. Albert's vision of financial empowerment. By making cryptocurrency accessible to people from all walks of life, Pi Network has the potential to bridge the gap between those who have traditionally had access to financial opportunities and those who have not.

For those new to the world of cryptocurrency, the concept of digital money can be intimidating. Terms like "blockchain," "mining," and "consensus algorithm" may sound complex, but as Joel has shown time and time again, complexity is no barrier to understanding.

This book is designed to demystify Pi Coin and its underlying technology, and to show you how it can be a powerful tool on your journey to financial freedom.

But what exactly is Pi Coin, and why should you care?

Chapter 1

Overview Of Cryptocurrency

The Evolution of Money

The concept of money has evolved over millennia, reflecting the changing needs, challenges, and innovations of human societies. From the simplest barter systems to the complex digital currencies of today, money has always been a central component of human interaction, facilitating trade, building economies, and driving growth. Understanding this evolution is crucial, especially as we stand on the threshold of a new era in financial technology with the advent of cryptocurrencies like PiCoin.

In the earliest days of human civilization, trade was conducted through barter, a system in which goods and services were directly exchanged without a standardized medium. This system worked in small, simple societies where individuals could easily find others who wanted what they had to offer and possessed something they wanted in return.

However, barter had significant limitations. The most obvious was the problem of "double coincidence of wants"—the need for both parties to want what the other was offering at the same time. As societies grew larger and more complex, these limitations became more apparent, and the inefficiencies of barter made it difficult to sustain larger-scale economic activity.

To address these challenges, early societies began to develop standardized forms of money that could be more widely accepted in exchange for goods and services. The first of these were commodities like grains, livestock, or shells, which had intrinsic value and could be used both as a medium of exchange and a store of value. Over time, as trade expanded and economies became more sophisticated, the limitations of commodity money became apparent. Livestock could die, and grains could spoil, which made them less reliable as stores of value.

This led to the invention of metal coins, which represented a significant leap forward in the evolution of money. Coins, typically made from precious metals like gold and silver, were durable, divisible, and had intrinsic value based on the metal content. They were widely accepted, and their use spread across different civilizations, facilitating trade over longer distances and between more diverse groups of people.

The introduction of coins also allowed for the accumulation and storage of wealth, which was essential for the development of more complex economic systems.

However, as economies continued to grow, even coins proved insufficient for the needs of expanding trade networks. The sheer volume of transactions in larger economies made it impractical to carry around large quantities of metal coins. This led to the development of paper currency, which represented a further evolution in the concept of money.

The earliest forms of paper money were promissory notes—essentially IOUs that could be exchanged for a certain amount of gold or silver. These notes were easier to transport and allowed for more efficient transactions. Over time, governments began to issue standardized paper currency, backed by the promise of redemption in gold or silver. This system, known as the gold standard, became the foundation of the modern monetary system.

The gold standard remained in place for centuries, but it, too, had its limitations. Economic growth, inflation, and the demands of modern economies eventually led to the abandonment of the gold standard in favor of fiat money—currency that has no intrinsic value but is accepted as legal tender by government decree. Today, most of the world's currencies are fiat money, and they function based on trust in the issuing governments and the stability of the economies they represent.

In recent decades, the rise of digital technology has begun to challenge even this long-established system. The advent of the internet and advances in computing power have paved the way for the development of digital currencies—forms of money that exist only in electronic form and are not tied to any physical commodity or government-issued currency.

Digital currencies offer a range of advantages, including lower transaction costs, faster transfer times, and the ability to conduct transactions across borders without the need for intermediaries like banks.

The development of digital currencies has been marked by several key milestones, beginning with the creation of e-money and virtual currencies in the late 20th century. These early forms of digital money were primarily used in online gaming and other niche markets.

However, they laid the groundwork for the emergence of cryptocurrencies—digital currencies that use cryptography to secure transactions and control the creation of new units.

The first and most well-known cryptocurrency, Bitcoin, was introduced in 2009 by an anonymous individual or group known as Satoshi Nakamoto. Bitcoin was revolutionary in that it combined existing concepts like cryptography, peer-to-peer networking, and blockchain technology to create a decentralized form of money that could be transferred directly between users without the need for a central authority.

Bitcoin's success inspired the creation of thousands of other cryptocurrencies, each with its own unique features and use cases. Blockchain technology, which underpins cryptocurrencies like Bitcoin and PiCoin, is arguably the most significant innovation in the history of money since the invention of coins.

A blockchain is a distributed ledger that records transactions across a network of computers, making it virtually impossible to alter or falsify the records. This transparency and security have made blockchain an attractive solution for a wide range of applications beyond just money, including supply chain management, voting systems, and digital identity verification.

The significance of blockchain technology lies in its ability to create trust in a system without the need for intermediaries. In traditional financial systems, trust is typically established through centralized institutions like banks, which act as intermediaries between parties in a transaction. These institutions are responsible for verifying transactions, preventing fraud, and ensuring that the system operates smoothly. However, this centralization also creates vulnerabilities, as seen in numerous financial crises where the failure of a single institution can have catastrophic consequences for the entire system.

Blockchain technology addresses these vulnerabilities by decentralizing the verification process. In a blockchain, transactions are validated by a network of nodes, each of which has a copy of the entire ledger. When a new transaction is added to the blockchain, it is broadcast to the network, and the nodes work together to validate it. Once a consensus is reached, the transaction is added to the blockchain, and it becomes a permanent part of the ledger.

This process makes it extremely difficult for any single party to manipulate the system, as doing so would require control of a majority of the network's computing power.

The decentralized nature of blockchain technology also makes it more resilient to attacks and failures. In a centralized system, an attack on the central authority can compromise the entire system. In contrast, a blockchain's distributed architecture ensures that even if some nodes are compromised, the system as a whole remains secure. This resilience has made blockchain an attractive option for a wide range of applications beyond just cryptocurrencies.

Blockchain's ability to create trust without intermediaries has profound implications for how we think about and use money. In a world where trust in traditional institutions is increasingly being questioned, blockchain offers a way to rebuild that trust on a more secure and transparent foundation. This has the potential to transform not only the financial industry but also many other sectors that rely on centralized systems for trust and verification.

As blockchain technology continues to evolve, it is likely to become an integral part of the global financial system. Already, we are seeing the development of new financial products and services built on blockchain, from decentralized finance (DeFi) platforms that allow users to lend, borrow, and trade assets without intermediaries, to stablecoins that are pegged to the value of traditional currencies and offer a more stable store of value.

For cryptocurrencies like PiCoin, blockchain technology is not just a technical innovation; it is the foundation of their value proposition. By enabling secure, transparent, and decentralized transactions, blockchain allows PiCoin to function as a medium of exchange, a store of value, and a platform for building new financial applications. PiCoin's focus on accessibility, with its mobile-first approach to mining, is a sign to the transformative potential of blockchain in making digital currencies more inclusive and widely adopted.

The journey from barter to blockchain represents a continuous evolution in the way we think about and use money. Each step in this evolution has been driven by the need to overcome the limitations of previous systems and to meet the changing demands of societies and economies. Today, as we stand on the brink of a new era in financial technology, it is clear that blockchain and cryptocurrencies will play a central role in shaping the future of money.

For those new to the world of digital currencies, understanding this evolution is key to appreciating the potential of cryptocurrencies like PiCoin. By tracing the history of money from its earliest forms to the cutting-edge technology of blockchain, we can see how each innovation has built on the lessons of the past to create more efficient, secure, and inclusive financial systems.

As you continue to explore the world of Cryptocurrency, PiCoin, and its blockchain technology, remember that this is not just about adopting a new form of money. It is about participating in a broader movement toward a more decentralized, transparent, and equitable financial system. Whether you are a beginner or an expert, a cryptocurrency enthusiast or a skeptic, understanding the evolution of money is the first step toward unlocking the full potential of this exciting new technology.

Key Takeaway: The evolution of money from barter to blockchain reflects humanity's ongoing quest to create more efficient, secure, and inclusive financial systems. Blockchain technology, as exemplified by cryptocurrencies like PiCoin, represents the latest and perhaps most significant step in this journey, offering a new model of trust and transparency in the digital age.

Understanding Digital Assets

In the rapidly evolving landscape of modern finance, digital assets have emerged as a transformative force, reshaping the way people view and interact with money. Digital assets, at their core, are representations of value that exist in electronic form. Unlike traditional financial assets such as stocks, bonds, or physical commodities, digital assets are created, stored, and transferred using digital technologies.

This distinction is crucial in understanding why they are not just an extension of existing financial systems but rather a new category that brings unique opportunities and challenges.

Digital assets encompass a broad range of instruments, from digital currencies like Bitcoin and PiCoin to tokenized representations of physical assets and intellectual property. What sets digital assets apart from traditional financial instruments is their reliance on decentralized technologies, particularly blockchain. These technologies enable the creation of assets that are not tied to any central authority, allowing for peer-to-peer transactions that are secure, transparent, and resistant to censorship.

The most prominent subset of digital assets is cryptocurrencies. Cryptocurrencies are digital or virtual currencies that use cryptography for security. They are designed to function as a medium of exchange, allowing users to conduct transactions without the need for intermediaries like banks. This peer-to-peer nature is one of the defining characteristics of cryptocurrencies, distinguishing them from traditional forms of money that rely on centralized institutions for issuance and regulation.

Cryptocurrencies like PiCoin represent a significant shift in how value can be transferred and stored. Unlike fiat currencies, which are backed by governments and subject to their monetary policies, cryptocurrencies operate on decentralized networks. These networks are often powered by blockchain technology, which serves as a public ledger for recording all transactions. The decentralized nature of blockchain ensures that no single entity has control over the currency, which is one of the factors contributing to the growing interest in cryptocurrencies as an alternative to traditional money.

The role of cryptocurrencies in the broader context of digital finance cannot be overstated. They are not just new forms of currency; they are the foundation of a larger ecosystem that includes various financial services, from decentralized finance (DeFi) platforms to digital wallets and payment systems. Cryptocurrencies enable new forms of financial interactions that were previously impossible or impractical.

For example, they allow for the creation of smart contracts—self-executing contracts with the terms of the agreement directly written into code. These contracts automatically execute when the specified conditions are met, reducing the need for intermediaries and lowering the cost of transactions.

In addition to their use as a medium of exchange, cryptocurrencies also function as a store of value. Some investors view cryptocurrencies as a hedge against inflation or as a way to diversify their portfolios. The limited supply of many cryptocurrencies, such as Bitcoin, contrasts with the unlimited printing of fiat currencies by central banks, which can lead to concerns about inflation. This scarcity factor has led some to liken cryptocurrencies to digital gold, a store of value that is not subject to the same inflationary pressures as traditional currencies.

However, while the potential benefits of digital assets and cryptocurrencies are significant, they are not without risks. The most immediate risk is volatility. Cryptocurrencies are known for their price fluctuations, which can be extreme over short periods. This volatility can be attributed to several factors, including market speculation, regulatory developments, and the relative novelty of the asset class. For investors, this volatility presents both opportunities and challenges, as the potential for high returns is accompanied by the risk of significant losses.

Another risk associated with digital assets is security. While blockchain technology is inherently secure due to its decentralized and cryptographic nature, the broader ecosystem of digital finance is still vulnerable to hacks, fraud, and other forms of cybercrime. Exchanges, where cryptocurrencies are often bought and sold, have been targets of high-profile attacks, resulting in the loss of millions of dollars' worth of digital assets. Additionally, the anonymity that some cryptocurrencies offer can be exploited for illicit activities, such as money laundering or financing illegal operations.

Regulatory uncertainty is another challenge facing digital assets. Because cryptocurrencies operate independently of traditional financial systems, they often fall outside the scope of existing regulations. This lack of regulatory clarity creates uncertainty for both users and investors. Governments around the world are grappling with how to regulate cryptocurrencies, balancing the need to protect consumers and prevent illegal activities with the desire to foster innovation in the financial sector. The regulatory environment is constantly evolving, and changes in policy can have a significant impact on the value and viability of digital assets.

Despite these risks, the benefits of digital assets, particularly cryptocurrencies, are driving widespread adoption and innovation. One of the most significant benefits is financial inclusion. Cryptocurrencies offer a way for people who are unbanked or underbanked to participate in the global economy.

In many parts of the world, access to traditional banking services is limited, either by geography or by cost. Cryptocurrencies, which only require an internet connection and a smartphone, provide an alternative that is accessible to a much broader population. This democratization of financial services has the potential to lift millions out of poverty by giving them access to tools for saving, investing, and transferring money.

Another benefit of digital assets is the efficiency they bring to financial transactions. Traditional financial systems are often slow, costly, and cumbersome, especially when dealing with cross-border transactions. Cryptocurrencies, by contrast, can be transferred quickly and at a lower cost, regardless of geographic location. This efficiency is not only beneficial for individuals but also for businesses, particularly those that operate in multiple countries or deal with high volumes of transactions. By reducing the time and cost associated with transferring money, cryptocurrencies can streamline operations and improve the bottom line.

Moreover, digital assets open up new opportunities for investment and wealth creation. In addition to buying and holding cryptocurrencies, individuals can participate in decentralized finance (DeFi) platforms that offer a range of financial services, including lending, borrowing, and trading, all without the need for traditional financial intermediaries. These platforms are built on blockchain technology and use smart contracts to automate transactions, making them more accessible and often more affordable than their traditional counterparts.

The possibilities for innovation in the digital asset realm are immense. New forms of digital assets are being created all the time, from non-fungible tokens (NFTs), which represent ownership of unique digital or physical items, to stablecoins, which are cryptocurrencies pegged to the value of traditional currencies to reduce volatility. These innovations are expanding the ways in which digital assets can be used and are creating new markets and opportunities for entrepreneurs, investors, and consumers alike.

In summary, digital assets represent a new era of finance that is characterized by decentralization, innovation, and accessibility. While they differ from traditional financial assets in significant ways, the potential they offer for transforming how value is created, stored, and transferred is immense.

Cryptocurrencies, as a subset of digital assets, are at the forefront of this transformation, offering new ways to conduct transactions, invest, and interact with financial services. Yet, like any emerging technology, it carries risks that require thoughtful consideration. Volatility, security concerns, and regulatory uncertainty are all challenges that must be addressed as the digital asset ecosystem continues to evolve.

As we move further into this new era of finance, it is essential to remain informed and cautious, balancing the potential benefits with an understanding of the risks. Whether you are a beginner or an experienced investor, the key to success in the digital asset space is education. By staying informed and understanding both the opportunities and the challenges, you can make more informed decisions and take advantage of the new possibilities that digital assets, including cryptocurrencies like Bitcoin and PiCoin, have to offer.

Key Takeaway: Digital assets, including cryptocurrencies, are reshaping the financial landscape by offering new ways to create, store, and transfer value. While they present significant opportunities for innovation and financial inclusion, it is crucial to understand the associated risks and to approach this emerging asset class with both curiosity and caution.

Chapter 2

The Rise of Pi Network

The Vision Behind Pi Network

The world of cryptocurrency has often been seen as a domain reserved for tech-savvy individuals with access to specialized hardware and extensive knowledge of blockchain technology. This perception has, for a long time, limited the accessibility and inclusivity of digital currencies, making it difficult for everyday people to participate. Recognizing these barriers, the Pi Network was conceived with a bold and inclusive mission: to democratize cryptocurrency, making it accessible to everyone, regardless of their technical expertise or financial means.

At the heart of the Pi Network's mission is the belief that the benefits of cryptocurrency should not be confined to a small, elite group of early adopters but should be available to all. The founders of Pi Network set out to create a digital currency that could be mined by anyone with a smartphone, without the need for expensive equipment or technical know-how. This vision of inclusivity is central to Pi Network's approach, as it seeks to level the playing field in a space that has historically been dominated by those with the resources to invest in high-powered mining rigs.

The concept of mobile mining is one of the key innovations that sets Pi Network apart from traditional cryptocurrencies like Bitcoin. In the early days of Bitcoin, mining was relatively straightforward and could be done using a personal computer. However, as the network grew and the difficulty of mining increased, it became necessary to invest in specialized hardware known as ASICs (Application-Specific Integrated Circuits) to compete effectively. This shift made it increasingly difficult for ordinary users to participate in the mining process, as the cost of entry skyrocketed.

In contrast, Pi Network introduced a revolutionary approach to mining that could be done on a mobile device, making it possible for anyone with a smartphone to mine PiCoin. This approach does not require the intense computational power needed for traditional mining, nor does it consume significant amounts of energy. Instead, mobile mining on the Pi Network is designed to be energy-efficient and user-friendly, allowing individuals to contribute to the network without incurring the high costs associated with traditional mining methods.

The Pi Network's mobile mining process is not only more accessible but also environmentally conscious. Traditional cryptocurrency mining has faced criticism for its energy consumption, with Bitcoin mining alone consuming more electricity than some entire countries. The Pi Network, by contrast, uses a consensus algorithm that is designed to be energy-efficient, minimizing its environmental impact. This focus on sustainability is part of the Pi Network's broader mission to create a cryptocurrency that is not only inclusive but also responsible in its use of resources.

The vision behind Pi Network is rooted in the belief that cryptocurrency can and should be a tool for empowerment, providing individuals with greater control over their financial futures. The founders of Pi Network, a group of Stanford graduates with backgrounds in computer science and social science, were motivated by a desire to address the inequities that have emerged in the cryptocurrency space. They recognized that while cryptocurrencies have the potential to transform the global financial system, their benefits have often been concentrated among those with the means to participate fully. By lowering the barriers to entry, the Pi Network aims to broaden participation and ensure that the advantages of cryptocurrency are more evenly distributed.

This vision aligns closely with the broader goals of the cryptocurrency community, which has long championed the principles of decentralization, transparency, and financial inclusion. From the early days of Bitcoin, the cryptocurrency movement has been driven by a desire to create a more equitable financial system, one that is less reliant on traditional intermediaries like banks and more open to individuals around the world. The Pi Network builds on these ideals by making it easier for people to join the network and benefit from its growth.

The founders of Pi Network have also placed a strong emphasis on community-building, recognizing that the success of any cryptocurrency depends not just on its technology but also on the strength and engagement of its user base. To this end, Pi Network has been designed with a focus on social interactions, encouraging users to invite friends and family to join the network and participate in the mining process. This approach has helped to create a vibrant and growing community of Pi Network users, who are actively engaged in the development and promotion of the network.

As the Pi Network continues to grow, it remains committed to its core mission of democratizing cryptocurrency. This commitment is reflected in the ongoing development of the network, which aims to provide users with new tools and features that enhance their ability to participate in the digital economy. From enabling peer-to-peer transactions to facilitating the development of decentralized applications (dApps) on the Pi blockchain, the Pi Network is focused on creating a comprehensive ecosystem that supports the needs of its users.

One of the key challenges facing the Pi Network as it moves forward is maintaining the balance between accessibility and security. Ensuring that the network remains open to new users while also protecting against potential threats is a top priority for the founders. To address this, the Pi Network employs a multi-layered security approach, including the use of cryptographic techniques and a consensus algorithm that prioritizes trust and validation within the network. These measures are designed to safeguard the integrity of the network while allowing it to scale effectively.

As the Pi Network progresses, it is poised to play a significant role in the ongoing evolution of the cryptocurrency space. By prioritizing accessibility, sustainability, and community engagement, the Pi Network is helping to redefine what it means to participate in the world of digital currencies.

Its innovative approach to mobile mining, coupled with its commitment to inclusivity, positions the Pi Network as a leader in the effort to bring the benefits of cryptocurrency to a broader audience.

The rise of Pi Network is a sign to the power of innovation and vision in driving change within the cryptocurrency space. By challenging the status quo and offering a new model for participation, the Pi Network is helping to pave the way for a more inclusive and equitable future for digital currencies. As more people around the world gain access to the tools and resources needed to engage with cryptocurrency, the impact of the Pi Network's mission will continue to grow, contributing to the broader goal of financial empowerment for all.

In summary, the Pi Network's mission to democratize cryptocurrency is rooted in the belief that everyone should have the opportunity to participate in the digital economy. Through its innovative approach to mobile mining and its focus on community-building, the Pi Network is making cryptocurrency more accessible and inclusive. As the network evolves, it remains committed to creating a secure and sustainable ecosystem that empowers individuals to take control of their financial futures.

Key Takeaway: Pi Network's mission to make cryptocurrency accessible to everyone, coupled with its innovative mobile mining approach, positions it as a trailblazer in the effort to democratize digital currencies and broaden financial inclusion.

The Founders and Their Mission

The Pi Network, one of the most ambitious projects in the cryptocurrency space, was born from the minds of three Stanford University graduates. These founders—Dr. Nicolas Kokkalis, Dr. Chengdiao Fan, and Vincent McPhillip—are not only academically distinguished but also driven by a shared vision of making cryptocurrency accessible to everyone. Their backgrounds in computer science, social computing, and management have been crucial in shaping the development of Pi Network, guiding it from a concept into a global phenomenon.

Dr. Nicolas Kokkalis, the brain behind the technical framework of Pi Network, holds a Ph.D. in computer science from Stanford. His expertise lies in decentralized applications and blockchain technology, making him uniquely qualified to lead the development of a cryptocurrency that aims to be inclusive and user-friendly. Kokkalis had already made significant contributions to the field of computer science, particularly in developing large-scale distributed systems and smart contracts. His deep understanding of these technologies became the foundation upon which Pi Network was built, ensuring that the network could scale while remaining accessible to users without technical backgrounds.

Dr. Chengdiao Fan, another key figure in the creation of Pi Network, brings a background in social computing and human-computer interaction. Her research at Stanford focused on how technology can foster social engagement and how it impacts society. This focus on the human aspect of technology is evident in Pi Network's design, which emphasizes community building and user involvement.

Fan's work has always revolved around the idea of empowering individuals through technology, and Pi Network is a natural extension of that philosophy, aiming to democratize access to cryptocurrency by making it as simple as downloading an app.

Vincent McPhillip, the third co-founder, complements the technical expertise of Kokkalis and Fan with his background in management and social impact. A graduate of Yale and Stanford, McPhillips' career has been dedicated to creating positive social change through technology and education.

His involvement in Pi Network has been instrumental in shaping its mission to bring cryptocurrency to the masses, focusing on how the network can provide real value to its users, particularly those who have been excluded from the traditional financial system. McPhillips' leadership in community engagement has helped Pi Network grow rapidly, fostering a user base that is both enthusiastic and diverse.

The journey of Pi Network began at Stanford, where the founders, driven by their academic and professional experiences, recognized the potential for blockchain technology to revolutionize not just finance but also the way people interact with digital systems. However, they also saw the barriers that prevented many from participating in this new digital economy—namely, the technical complexity and high costs associated with traditional cryptocurrency mining.

It was this realization that led them to conceptualize a new kind of cryptocurrency, one that could be mined on a smartphone and used by anyone, anywhere in the world. The path from concept to reality was neither straightforward nor easy. Developing a cryptocurrency that could be mined on mobile devices required overcoming significant technical challenges. Traditional blockchain networks rely on proof-of-work consensus mechanisms, which demand immense computational power and energy.

The Pi Network team needed to design a new consensus algorithm that would be secure, scalable, and efficient enough to run on everyday smartphones without draining their batteries or requiring advanced technical knowledge from users. This challenge was a major milestone in Pi Network's development, as it required the team to rethink many of the assumptions underlying existing blockchain technologies.

Another significant challenge was ensuring the network's security while maintaining its accessibility. The Pi Network's consensus algorithm, known as the Stellar Consensus Protocol (SCP), was chosen for its ability to provide security without the need for intensive computational resources. Implementing SCP into a mobile-friendly format was a complex process, requiring extensive testing and iteration to ensure that it could handle the demands of a growing user base while protecting against potential threats.

This step was crucial in establishing the credibility of Pi Network as a legitimate and secure cryptocurrency.

The launch of Pi Network was a carefully planned process, starting with a beta phase that allowed the team to refine the network based on user feedback. This phase was critical in identifying and addressing any issues that arose, ensuring that the network could scale effectively as more users joined.

The founders understood the importance of building a strong community around Pi Network, so they emphasized the role of early adopters in shaping the future of the project. This approach not only helped in debugging and improving the system but also created a sense of ownership and involvement among the network's users, who felt that they were part of something groundbreaking.

As Pi Network moved from its beta phase to a wider launch, the team faced new challenges, including how to sustain the network's growth while maintaining its core principles of accessibility and decentralization. The rapid increase in user numbers required scaling the network's infrastructure, which involved significant logistical and technical efforts. The team also had to navigate the complexities of introducing Pi Network to a global audience, which meant addressing diverse regulatory environments, cultural differences, and varying levels of digital literacy.

One of the key milestones in Pi Network's development was the introduction of KYC (Know Your Customer) procedures, a necessary step to comply with global regulations and ensure that the network could transition from its early stages into a fully operational cryptocurrency. Implementing KYC was a complex and resource-intensive process, requiring the team to build a system that could handle the verification of millions of users while protecting their privacy and security.

This step was crucial in preparing Pi Network for its eventual integration into the broader financial system, enabling users to trade PiCoin on exchanges and use it in real-world transactions.

Throughout these challenges, the founders remained committed to their original mission: to create a cryptocurrency that was truly for the people.

Their journey from Stanford to launching Pi Network globally is an evidence to the power of innovation, determination, and a clear vision. Despite the obstacles they encountered, the team's dedication to democratizing access to cryptocurrency never wavered. They understood that to achieve their goal, they needed to build not just a technically sound product but also a strong and engaged community that believed in the project's potential.

Today, Pi Network stands as a unique entity in the cryptocurrency world, with millions of users around the globe mining PiCoin on their smartphones. This success is a direct result of the founders' ability to translate their academic insights and professional experiences into a product that resonates with a broad audience. By making cryptocurrency accessible and user-friendly, they have opened the door for millions of people to participate in the digital economy, many for the first time.

The journey of Pi Network, from an idea at Stanford to a global movement, highlights the importance of perseverance and innovation in the face of challenges. The founders' ability to adapt and evolve the network in response to user needs and technological advances has been critical to its success. As Pi Network continues to grow, it remains guided by the same principles that inspired its creation: inclusivity, accessibility, and the belief that cryptocurrency can be a tool for empowerment.

In summary, the story of Pi Network is not just about the development of a new cryptocurrency but about the vision of its founders to create something that could bring real value to people around the world. Their journey from Stanford to smartphones is a sign to their commitment to innovation, inclusivity, and the power of community. By overcoming the challenges they faced and staying true to their mission, the founders of Pi Network have made significant strides toward their goal of democratizing cryptocurrency.

Key Takeaway: The founders of Pi Network, with their strong academic and professional backgrounds, have successfully translated their vision of an accessible and inclusive cryptocurrency into reality, overcoming numerous challenges along the way. Their journey underscores the importance of innovation, community, and commitment in creating a digital currency that truly serves the people.

Chapter 3

How Pi Cryptocurrency Works

The Pi Mining Process

The Pi cryptocurrency represents a groundbreaking shift in the way digital currencies are mined, making it possible for anyone with a smartphone to participate in the process. Unlike traditional cryptocurrencies, which rely on resource-intensive methods to validate transactions and secure the network, Pi has been designed from the ground up to be lightweight and energy-efficient, with accessibility as a core principle. This unique approach to mining, known as mobile mining, allows users to contribute to the network without the need for expensive hardware or a deep understanding of blockchain technology.

The mining process for Pi coins is fundamentally different from the proof-of-work (PoW) mechanisms used by many other cryptocurrencies. In a typical PoW system, miners compete to solve complex mathematical problems, a process that requires substantial computational power and consumes vast amounts of energy.

This has led to concerns about the environmental impact of cryptocurrencies like Bitcoin, which rely on such energy-intensive processes. Pi, on the other hand, uses a consensus algorithm called the Stellar Consensus Protocol (SCP), which does not require miners to solve computational puzzles. Instead, Pi's system is based on trust circles and user validation, allowing it to operate with minimal energy consumption.

In practice, this means that Pi coins can be mined using the processing power of a smartphone without draining its battery or affecting its performance. When a user logs into the Pi Network app, they can start mining simply by tapping a button. The process runs in the background and does not involve the kind of heavy data processing that characterizes traditional mining.

Instead, the app verifies that the user is a legitimate participant in the network by checking their connection to other trusted members. This approach not only reduces the computational load but also ensures that the network remains secure and decentralized.

Making cryptocurrency mining accessible through smartphones has significant implications for the broader adoption of digital currencies. Traditionally, mining has been an activity reserved for those with the financial resources and technical skills to set up and maintain powerful mining rigs. This has led to the concentration of mining power in the hands of a relatively small number of individuals and organizations, which runs counter to the decentralized ethos of cryptocurrency.

By lowering the barriers to entry, Pi Network allows a much wider range of people to participate in the creation and distribution of digital currency. This democratization of mining has the potential to bring cryptocurrency into the mainstream, as more people become directly involved in the network.

One of the most common questions about mobile mining is whether it is truly effective and secure compared to traditional methods.

Skeptics often wonder how a process that runs on a smartphone can possibly compete with the high-powered mining farms that dominate other cryptocurrencies. The key difference lies in the design of the network. Pi's SCP-based consensus mechanism is not about who can solve the most difficult problems the fastest but rather about building a network of trust among users. Each participant in the Pi Network plays a role in validating transactions and maintaining the integrity of the blockchain, creating a system that is secure yet requires far less energy than traditional mining.

Another misconception about mobile mining is that it might be less rewarding or slower than traditional mining methods. In the Pi Network, the rewards are designed to incentivize early adopters and those who actively contribute to the growth and security of the network.

While the mining rate for Pi decreases as the network grows, this is a deliberate feature to ensure the currency remains scarce and valuable over time. Users are rewarded not just for their own mining activity but also for the trust and connections they build within the network. This approach aligns the incentives of individual miners with the health of the overall network, promoting long-term engagement rather than short-term profit.

Pi Network's mobile mining also addresses the environmental concerns associated with traditional mining.

The energy consumption of cryptocurrencies like Bitcoin has been a major point of criticism, with some estimates suggesting that Bitcoin mining alone uses more electricity than some entire countries. By contrast, Pi's approach to mining is designed to be as energy-efficient as possible, making it a more sustainable option for those concerned about the ecological impact of digital currencies.

Since the mining process does not rely on energy-intensive computations, it can be carried out without contributing to the growing problem of carbon emissions from blockchain technology.

For beginners, one of the appealing aspects of Pi's mining process is its simplicity. Unlike other cryptocurrencies, where setting up a mining operation can be a daunting task requiring specialized knowledge and equipment, Pi's mining process is as straightforward as using a mobile app. This ease of use is a crucial factor in making cryptocurrency more accessible to a broader audience. As more people around the world gain access to smartphones, the potential user base for Pi Network expands, further driving the growth and adoption of the currency.

However, it's important to note that while mobile mining is more accessible and environmentally friendly, it also requires a different mindset compared to traditional mining. The rewards may be smaller on a per-user basis, especially as the network grows and the mining rate decreases.

But the focus of Pi Network is on building a strong, engaged community rather than just on generating profits. This community-driven approach is what sets Pi apart and could be the key to its long-term success.

As with any new technology, there are still questions and uncertainties about how Pi Network will evolve and how its mining process will hold up as the network scales. The founders of Pi Network are aware of these challenges and are continually working to improve the system and address any issues that arise.

In summary, Pi cryptocurrency's mobile mining process represents a significant innovation in the world of digital currencies. By making mining accessible to anyone with a smartphone, Pi Network has opened up the possibility of cryptocurrency to a much broader audience. Its lightweight, energy-efficient design challenges the traditional notions of mining, offering a more sustainable and inclusive model for the future of digital currency. As the network continues to grow, it will be interesting to see how this approach influences the broader cryptocurrency ecosystem and whether it can truly democratize access to digital money.

Key Takeaway: Pi's mobile mining process offers an accessible, energy-efficient alternative to traditional cryptocurrency mining, making it possible for anyone with a smartphone to participate in the network and contribute to the growth of digital currency.

Pi's Consensus Algorithm

The Pi Network is built on a foundation of innovative technology, with the Stellar Consensus Protocol (SCP) playing a central role in how its blockchain operates. SCP, originally designed for the Stellar network, provides a way for decentralized networks to reach agreement, or consensus, on the state of the blockchain in a secure and efficient manner.

This protocol differs significantly from other well-known consensus mechanisms, such as Proof of Work (PoW) and Proof of Stake (PoS), by focusing on energy efficiency, scalability, and inclusivity, which align perfectly with Pi's mission to make cryptocurrency accessible to a broader audience.

At its core, the Stellar Consensus Protocol operates on the principle of federated Byzantine agreement (FBA). Unlike PoW, which requires miners to solve complex computational puzzles, or PoS, which depends on the amount of cryptocurrency a participant holds, SCP relies on the agreement between nodes within the network. Each node, which can be thought of as a participant in the network, selects a group of other nodes it trusts, forming what is known as a quorum slice.

When these quorum slices overlap, consensus is achieved without the need for every node in the network to directly interact with every other node.
This process significantly reduces the energy consumption required to maintain the blockchain and enables the network to scale effectively as more participants join.

For the Pi Network, SCP's design is particularly advantageous because it allows for the inclusion of participants who are not running energy-intensive hardware. This is in stark contrast to PoW, which has faced criticism for its high energy demands and the resulting environmental impact. In PoW systems like Bitcoin, miners compete to solve cryptographic puzzles, with the first to solve it receiving a reward in the form of newly minted coins. This competition drives the need for increasingly powerful and energy-hungry mining rigs, which centralizes mining power among those who can afford the necessary hardware and electricity costs.

Pi's adoption of SCP eliminates this need for competition, as consensus is achieved through trust and cooperation among nodes rather than brute computational force.
When compared to Proof of Stake, which selects validators based on the number of coins they hold, SCP offers a more egalitarian approach.

PoS can lead to a concentration of power among those who already hold large amounts of the cryptocurrency, as their holdings give them more influence over the network's operations. This can create barriers for new participants who may find it difficult to acquire enough cryptocurrency to have a meaningful impact. SCP, on the other hand, does not require participants to hold large amounts of Pi to contribute to the consensus process. Instead, it emphasizes the importance of trust relationships and social connections within the network, allowing for a more decentralized and community-driven approach to maintaining the blockchain.

One of the key advantages of SCP in the context of Pi Network is its ability to scale without sacrificing security or decentralization. As more participants join the network and establish trust relationships, the consensus process becomes more robust, with the overlapping quorum slices ensuring that agreement can still be reached even in the presence of malicious or faulty nodes.

This is particularly important for Pi, which aims to bring cryptocurrency to a global audience, including those who may not have access to the resources needed to participate in more traditional blockchain networks. By leveraging SCP, Pi can accommodate a large number of users without the need for specialized hardware or high energy consumption, making it possible for anyone with a smartphone to contribute to the network.

However, while SCP offers significant advantages, it also comes with potential limitations. One challenge is ensuring that the network remains secure as it scales. In a system that relies on trust relationships, there is always the risk that these relationships could be manipulated or that malicious actors could attempt to exploit the system by gaining the trust of other nodes.

To mitigate this risk, Pi Network must continually monitor and update its security protocols, ensuring that the consensus process remains robust even as the network grows and evolves. Additionally, the reliance on trust relationships means that the quality of the network's consensus process is heavily dependent on the behavior of its participants. If users do not take care in selecting trustworthy nodes, the overall security of the network could be compromised.

Another potential limitation of SCP is its reliance on quorum slices for achieving consensus. While this system is efficient and scalable, it also introduces a degree of complexity that may be difficult for new users to understand. Unlike PoW or PoS, where the mechanics of the consensus process are relatively straightforward, SCP's federated Byzantine agreement requires a deeper understanding of how trust relationships and quorum slices interact to secure the network.

For Pi Network, which aims to make cryptocurrency accessible to a broad audience, this complexity could be a barrier to entry for some users. To address this, Pi must focus on educating its community about how SCP works and why it is an effective and secure method for achieving consensus.

Despite these challenges, the Stellar Consensus Protocol remains a powerful tool for Pi Network's mission of democratizing cryptocurrency. Its emphasis on energy efficiency, scalability, and decentralization aligns with Pi's goal of creating a cryptocurrency that is truly accessible to everyone. By leveraging SCP, Pi can build a network that is not only secure and robust but also capable of supporting a large and diverse user base. This sets Pi apart from other cryptocurrencies that rely on more traditional consensus mechanisms, offering a new model for how blockchain technology can be used to create value and build trust in a decentralized world.

In summary, Pi's use of the Stellar Consensus Protocol is a key component of its strategy to create a more inclusive and accessible cryptocurrency. By focusing on trust relationships and cooperation rather than competition and resource consumption, Pi is able to offer a secure and scalable blockchain that can be used by anyone with a smartphone. While there are challenges associated with this approach, particularly in terms of security and complexity, the potential benefits of SCP in the context of Pi Network are significant. As the network continues to grow and evolve, it will be important for Pi to address these challenges head-on, ensuring that its consensus process remains secure, efficient, and accessible to all.

Key Takeaway: The Stellar Consensus Protocol provides Pi Network with a secure, scalable, and energy-efficient method for achieving consensus, making it possible for anyone to participate in the blockchain without the need for specialized hardware or significant financial resources.

Chapter 4

Blockchain Technology Simplified

What is Blockchain?

Blockchain technology, often considered the backbone of cryptocurrencies, is a digital ledger that records transactions across a network of computers. Unlike traditional ledgers kept by banks or financial institutions, a blockchain is decentralized, meaning no single entity owns or controls it.

Each participant in the network holds a copy of the ledger, ensuring that every transaction is transparent, secure, and nearly impossible to alter.

Fundamentally, blockchain consists of a chain of blocks, each holding a record of transactions. These blocks are linked, or "chained," together in chronological order, creating an unbroken record of all activity on the network. Each block includes a unique code called a hash, which is generated using the information within the block and the hash of the previous block.

This connection between blocks ensures the integrity of the data; if someone tries to alter a block, its hash would change, breaking the chain and alerting the network to the tampering attempt.
Blockchain technology forms the foundation for cryptocurrencies like Bitcoin, Ethereum, and Pi by providing a decentralized system for recording and verifying transactions.

In traditional financial systems, banks and payment processors act as intermediaries, verifying transactions and maintaining records. This centralized model can be slow, expensive, and prone to fraud or errors. Blockchain eliminates the need for intermediaries by allowing participants to transact directly with one another, with the network itself validating and recording each transaction.

For Bitcoin, the first and most well-known cryptocurrency, blockchain enables peer-to-peer transactions without the need for a central authority. When someone sends Bitcoin, the transaction is broadcast to the network, where miners compete to validate it by solving complex mathematical puzzles. Once a miner successfully verifies the transaction, it is added to a new block, which is then appended to the blockchain. This process ensures that all participants agree on the state of the ledger, preventing double-spending and ensuring the security of the network.

Ethereum, another major cryptocurrency, also relies on blockchain technology, but with a focus on enabling smart contracts. These are self-executing contracts where the terms are written directly into code. When certain conditions are met, the contract automatically executes without the need for intermediaries. Ethereum's blockchain supports these contracts, enabling a wide range of decentralized applications, or dApps, to run on its network. This flexibility has made Ethereum the platform of choice for developers looking to create blockchain-based applications beyond simple transactions.

Pi, a newer entrant in the cryptocurrency space, uses blockchain technology in a way that emphasizes accessibility and ease of use. While Bitcoin and Ethereum rely on energy-intensive mining processes, Pi aims to democratize access to cryptocurrency by allowing users to mine coins using their smartphones.

Pi's blockchain operates on the principles of decentralization, transparency, and security, ensuring that transactions are recorded accurately and that all participants have a say in how the network is governed.

One of the key features of blockchain technology is decentralization. In a decentralized system, control is distributed across the network rather than being concentrated in the hands of a single entity. This reduces the risk of fraud, censorship, or manipulation, as there is no central authority that can alter the ledger. Decentralization also makes the network more resilient to attacks, as compromising one node (or computer) does not give an attacker control over the entire system.

For cryptocurrencies, decentralization is a core principle, as it allows users to transact freely without relying on banks, governments, or other intermediaries.
Transparency is another crucial aspect of blockchain technology. Because each participant in the network holds a copy of the blockchain, all transactions are visible to everyone.

This transparency ensures that the system operates fairly and that users can verify the integrity of the ledger. In traditional financial systems, transactions are often opaque, with records accessible only to a select few. Blockchain's open nature provides a level of accountability and trust that is difficult to achieve with centralized systems.

Immutability, or the inability to alter past records, is perhaps the most important feature of blockchain technology. Once a transaction is recorded in a block and added to the blockchain, it cannot be changed or deleted. This immutability is achieved through cryptographic hashing and the structure of the blockchain itself.

If someone tries to alter a transaction, the hash of the block would change, disrupting the chain and revealing the tampering attempt. This ensures that the blockchain remains a reliable and accurate record of all transactions, providing security and trust for users.

In the context of cryptocurrencies, these features of blockchain—decentralization, transparency, and immutability—are what make the technology so powerful. They allow for the creation of a secure, trustless system where users can transact directly with one another without the need for intermediaries.

This not only reduces costs and increases efficiency but also opens up new possibilities for financial inclusion, particularly in areas where traditional banking services are lacking.

For Pi, leveraging blockchain technology allows the network to fulfill its mission of creating a cryptocurrency that is accessible to everyone. By using a decentralized system, Pi ensures that all participants have an equal say in the network's operations. The transparency of the blockchain allows users to trust the system, knowing that all transactions are recorded accurately and that no single entity can manipulate the ledger. And with immutability, Pi provides a secure and reliable platform for users to transact, build trust, and create value.

In summary, blockchain technology is the foundation that enables cryptocurrencies like Bitcoin, Ethereum, and Pi to operate securely and efficiently. Its key features—decentralization, transparency, and immutability—provide the necessary infrastructure for a trustless system where users can transact without the need for intermediaries. As cryptocurrencies continue to evolve and gain adoption, the principles of blockchain will remain central to their success, offering new opportunities for financial innovation and inclusion.

Key Takeaway: Blockchain technology provides the secure, decentralized, and transparent foundation that makes cryptocurrencies possible, revolutionizing how transactions are recorded and verified without the need for intermediaries.

How Pi's Blockchain Differs

Pi Network's blockchain is designed with a clear focus on accessibility and efficiency, making it fundamentally different from the more resource-intensive blockchains that power cryptocurrencies like Bitcoin and Ethereum. One of the most distinctive aspects of Pi's blockchain is its lightweight nature, specifically tailored for mobile devices.

This approach stems from the belief that cryptocurrency should be available to everyone, regardless of their access to high-powered computing resources.

At the core of Pi's design is the need to minimize the computational and energy demands typically associated with blockchain networks.

Unlike Bitcoin and Ethereum, which rely on Proof of Work (PoW) and Proof of Stake (PoS) mechanisms respectively, Pi Network uses the Stellar Consensus Protocol (SCP).

This consensus mechanism was chosen specifically because it allows for secure, scalable, and decentralized operations without requiring extensive processing power or energy consumption. SCP enables Pi's blockchain to be lightweight by eliminating the need for traditional mining, which is a process where participants compete to solve complex mathematical puzzles to validate transactions.

Mining in PoW systems like Bitcoin is notoriously energy-intensive, requiring specialized hardware and significant electricity. This not only limits participation to those with substantial resources but also has raised environmental concerns due to the vast amounts of energy consumed(Mentioned Earlier).
Pi's choice of SCP allows the network to operate efficiently on mobile devices, ensuring that the barrier to entry is low and the system remains inclusive.

One of the key design choices in Pi's blockchain is its focus on mobile-first accessibility. The Pi Network team recognized early on that the future of cryptocurrency adoption hinges on reaching a broad audience, many of whom primarily access the internet through their smartphones.

By optimizing the blockchain for mobile devices, Pi makes it possible for users to participate in the network without needing to invest in expensive hardware. This mobile-first approach also aligns with the global trend towards mobile internet usage, particularly in regions where access to traditional computing devices is limited.

To maintain security while ensuring the blockchain remains lightweight, Pi Network balances several factors. First, the network relies on trust relationships between participants to validate transactions. Each user selects a trusted group of individuals within the network, and these trust circles overlap to form a consensus on the state of the blockchain. This method, which is intrinsic to SCP, reduces the need for intensive computational processes while still ensuring that the network remains secure against attacks.

By distributing trust across a wide network of participants, Pi can prevent any single entity from gaining control over the system. Scalability is another critical aspect of Pi's blockchain design. As the network grows, it must be able to handle an increasing number of transactions without compromising speed or security. The SCP allows for rapid consensus without the bottlenecks associated with traditional blockchain technologies.

In PoW systems, as more transactions are processed, the time and energy required to validate them increases, leading to slower transaction times and higher fees. Pi's blockchain, however, is designed to scale efficiently, making it possible for the network to expand without the growing pains experienced by other blockchains.

Accessibility is also a cornerstone of Pi's blockchain strategy. By reducing the complexity of participation, Pi opens the door for a more diverse user base. This is a marked difference from blockchains like Bitcoin and Ethereum, where the technical expertise required to participate can be a significant barrier.

With Pi, users can easily mine Pi coins on their smartphones with just a few taps, without needing to understand the intricate details of blockchain technology. This simplicity is key to Pi's goal of democratizing cryptocurrency, ensuring that anyone, regardless of technical knowledge or financial resources, can take part in the network.

Comparing Pi's blockchain to more resource-intensive ones like Bitcoin and Ethereum highlights the trade-offs and innovations inherent in Pi's approach. Bitcoin's blockchain, built on PoW, is robust and secure but comes at a high cost in terms of energy and resources. The competitive nature of PoW means that as more miners join the network, the difficulty of mining increases, leading to higher energy consumption and a concentration of mining power among those with the most resources. This can result in centralization, where a few large mining operations hold significant influence over the network.

Ethereum's blockchain, while shifting towards a PoS mechanism with Ethereum 2.0, still faces challenges related to scalability and energy use. PoS reduces the need for energy-intensive mining, but it can lead to centralization as those with more cryptocurrency have more influence over the network.

Additionally, Ethereum's smart contract functionality, while powerful, adds complexity to the network, which can result in slower transaction times and higher fees as the network becomes more congested.

In contrast, Pi's blockchain is designed to avoid these pitfalls by prioritizing energy efficiency and decentralization through SCP. The lack of traditional mining ensures that participation is not limited by access to expensive hardware, and the use of trust circles fosters a more community-driven approach to consensus. This model not only makes Pi more accessible but also more sustainable in the long term, as it avoids the escalating resource demands seen in other blockchain networks.

However, the lightweight nature of Pi's blockchain does come with its own set of challenges. The reliance on trust circles, while efficient, requires a strong and engaged user base to function effectively. If users do not carefully select their trust circles, the security of the network could be compromised.

Additionally, the focus on mobile accessibility, while inclusive, may limit the complexity of transactions that the network can handle compared to more robust blockchains like Ethereum. These are trade-offs that the Pi Network team continues to address as the network evolves.

In summary, Pi's blockchain represents a significant shift in how cryptocurrency networks can be designed. By focusing on lightweight, mobile-friendly technology, Pi has created a blockchain that is accessible, scalable, and secure without the resource-intensive demands of traditional systems like Bitcoin and Ethereum.

This approach opens up new possibilities for cryptocurrency adoption, particularly in regions and demographics that have been excluded from more traditional blockchain networks. As Pi continues to grow, its innovative use of SCP and commitment to accessibility will likely serve as a model for future blockchain projects.

Key Takeaway: Pi Network's lightweight, mobile-friendly blockchain design, leveraging the Stellar Consensus Protocol, offers a more accessible and sustainable alternative to traditional, resource-intensive blockchain systems.

Chapter 5

Getting Started with Pi Network

Setting Up Your Pi Account

(A Step-by-Step Guide)

To get started with Pi Network, the first step is downloading the Pi Network app, which is available on both iOS and Android platforms.

Head to the App Store or Google Play Store, search for "Pi Network," and select the official app developed by SocialChain. Download and install the app just like any other application. Once installed, open the app and you'll be greeted with an introductory screen explaining the basics of Pi Network.

This screen gives a brief overview of the project and its goals, which is helpful for new users who might be unfamiliar with how Pi operates.

After reviewing the introduction, you will be prompted to create an account. You have two options for signing up:
1. using your phone number.
2. Using your Facebook account.

If you choose to sign up with your phone number, ensure that you enter a valid number that you have access to, as you will need it for account verification. If you opt to sign up with Facebook, make sure that your Facebook account is secure and linked to an email address you use frequently.

This choice is crucial, as it ties your Pi account to an identity, which is important for security and future features like verifying your real identity on the network.
Once you've selected your signup method, you'll need to enter your name.

It's important to use your real name as it appears on your government-issued ID, as Pi Network implements a KYC (Know Your Customer) process to verify users' identities. This step is essential to ensure that the network remains secure and that all users are genuine participants. After entering your name, you'll be asked to create a username.

This is how you'll be identified on the network by other users, so choose something memorable but not too personal.

Securing your account with a strong password is the next critical step. Pi Network, like any other online platform, requires a secure password to protect your account from unauthorized access.

Select a password that is at least eight characters long, combining letters, numbers, and symbols. Avoid using easily guessable passwords like "123456" or "password." Instead, opt for something unique that you haven't used on other platforms. If you're worried about forgetting your password, consider using a password manager to keep it safe and accessible.

In addition to creating a strong password, it's recommended that you enable additional authentication methods to further secure your account. While Pi Network may not yet offer two-factor authentication(which I believe they'll in the future) as some other services do, it's good practice to stay updated on any security features the app might introduce in the future.

Keep your account credentials private, and never share your login information with anyone, as this could compromise the security of your Pi coins and personal information.

Once your account is set up and secured, you'll be introduced to the Pi Network app's main features. The home screen is where you'll see your current Pi balance and the rate at which you are mining Pi coins.To start mining, you'll need to tap the lightning bolt icon.

This begins the 24-hour mining session, after which you'll need to open the app and tap the icon again to continue mining. Mining on Pi Network is not resource-intensive; it doesn't drain your battery or use your phone's processing power, making it an easy task to perform daily.

Understanding the different roles in the Pi Network is essential for maximizing your mining potential. The app introduces you to three roles:
1. Pioneer.
2. Contributor.
3. Ambassador.

As a Pioneer, you're a basic user who mines Pi by checking in daily.

To become a Contributor, you'll need to build a security circle by inviting people you trust to the network and verifying their identity. This role allows you to mine at a higher rate because you're helping to secure the network.

The Ambassador role is for users who invite new members to join Pi Network using their referral code. For each person who joins using your code, your mining rate increases slightly, rewarding you for expanding the network.

The Pi Network app also features a chat function where you can communicate with other users in your country or region. This feature is particularly useful for discussing Pi-related topics, sharing tips, or seeking help if you encounter issues within the app. Engaging with the community can also provide insights into how others are using the app and what they expect from the network's future developments.

Another important feature within the Pi Network app is the "Earn Pi" section, which provides various ways to increase your Pi balance. Aside from mining, you can earn Pi by participating in Pi Network's ecosystem, which may include activities like sharing content, verifying other users, or participating in Pi-based apps and services as the network grows.

The "Pi Browser," available within the app, is another key feature that allows you to access decentralized applications (dApps) that are built on the Pi Network. This browser is intended to expand Pi's usability by connecting users to a variety of blockchain-based services directly from their phones.

The app includes an "Announcements" section where the Pi Core Team shares updates about new features, upcoming events, and other important information. Regularly checking this section will keep you informed about the progress of the network and how you can participate in new initiatives.

It's crucial to stay updated with the latest news and developments about Pi Network.

For users looking to deepen their involvement in Pi Network, understanding the roadmap and future plans is key.
The Pi Core Team has outlined several phases in the development of the network, which is currently moving towards the Mainnet launch.

The transition to Mainnet is a significant milestone where Pi coins will gain real value and be used in transactions. During this phase, users who have accumulated Pi coins can start trading, using, or spending them within the network's ecosystem.

As with any digital asset, it's important to approach Pi Network with a clear understanding of its goals and limitations. While the project has ambitious plans to create a widely accessible cryptocurrency, its success will depend on a variety of factors, including community support, technological developments, and regulatory considerations.

To sum up, getting started with Pi Network is straightforward and designed with accessibility in mind. By downloading the app, setting up a secure account, and familiarizing yourself with its features, you can begin mining Pi coins with minimal effort.

The app's user-friendly interface makes it easy for anyone and everyone, regardless of technical expertise, to participate in the cryptocurrency space. As the network evolves, staying informed and actively participating in the community will help you make the most of your Pi Network experience.

Key Takeaway: Setting up and securing your Pi Network account is the first step toward engaging with a new, accessible cryptocurrency that aims to bring blockchain technology to a broader audience.

If you're among those who haven't mined Pi Coin, download the pi coin app now via the QR code below.
Sign up using the invitation code provided and start mining.

Building Your Pi Network

(Referrals and Security Circles)

In the Pi Network, the concept of Security Circles is central to its unique approach to securing the network.

Unlike traditional cryptocurrencies that rely on energy-intensive methods like Proof of Work, Pi Network introduces a lightweight and user-friendly mechanism that allows everyday users to contribute to the network's security.

A Security Circle is essentially a group of trusted individuals within the Pi Network who vouch for each other's authenticity. Each user can add up to five people to their Security Circle, creating a web of trust that strengthens the overall security of the network.

The idea behind Security Circles is to leverage the power of personal relationships to enhance the integrity of the network. When you add someone to your Security

Circle, you're essentially saying that you trust this person not to act maliciously within the network. This trust is the foundation upon which Pi Network's security model is built. The more people you have in your Security Circle, the more secure the network becomes, as it becomes increasingly difficult for bad actors to infiltrate and disrupt the system.

Building a Security Circle isn't just about adding as many people as possible; it's about choosing the right people. It's crucial to add individuals you know personally and trust to act in the best interest of the network. These could be family members, close friends, or colleagues who share your enthusiasm for Pi Network.

By carefully selecting the members of your Security Circle, you contribute to the creation of a robust and reliable network that can resist attacks and maintain the integrity of transactions.

In addition to enhancing network security, Security Circles also play a role in improving your mining rate. The more people you have in your Security Circle, the higher your mining rate will be. This is Pi Network's way of incentivizing users to actively participate in securing the network.

However, it's important to note that the quality of your Security Circle is just as important as its quantity. A small group of highly trusted individuals can be more valuable than a large group of people you barely know. This is why it's essential to focus on building a strong and trustworthy Security Circle, rather than just adding as many people as possible.

Referrals are another key component of building your Pi Network. When you refer someone to join the network, you're helping to expand the Pi community and increase the network's overall security. Every time a new member joins using your referral code, your mining rate increases slightly. This is Pi

Network's way of rewarding users for spreading the word and bringing new people into the fold. However, referrals aren't just about increasing your mining rate; they're also about building a community of like-minded individuals who share your interest in Pi Network and its potential.

To maximize the benefits of referrals, it's important to be strategic about who you invite to join the network. Focus on inviting people who are genuinely interested in cryptocurrency and who are likely to remain active participants in the network. These individuals are more likely to contribute positively to the community and help build a stronger and more secure network.

Additionally, encouraging your referrals to create their own Security Circles can further enhance the security of the network and increase everyone's mining rate.
Building a strong and trustworthy Security Circle requires careful planning and a focus on quality over quantity.

Start by inviting people you know well and who you believe will be active and responsible members of the network. As your Security Circle grows, continue to assess its strength and consider removing members who aren't contributing positively. By maintaining a high-quality Security Circle, you'll not only enhance your own mining rate but also contribute to the overall security and stability of the Pi Network.

In summary, Security Circles and referrals are two fundamental aspects of building a successful Pi Network. By carefully selecting the members of your Security Circle and strategically inviting new members to join the network, you can help create a secure and thriving community that benefits everyone involved.

Chapter 6

The Pi Ecosystem

Pi as a Medium of Exchange (Potential Use Cases)

PiCoin, the native currency of the Pi Network, holds the potential to serve as a medium of exchange within its growing ecosystem and beyond. As the network continues to develop, there are various possibilities for how Pi could be used to facilitate transactions, offering a glimpse into the future of decentralized finance.

At its core, Pi is designed to be accessible, inclusive, and practical for everyday use, making it well-suited to serve as a digital currency for a wide range of applications.

One of the primary use cases for Pi as a currency lies within the Pi Network itself. As the network expands and more users join, a robust internal economy could emerge where Pi is exchanged for goods and services among community members.

This internal economy could take various forms, such as peer-to-peer transactions for digital content, freelance services, or even physical products. The simplicity and accessibility of Pi's mobile-based mining process make it an ideal candidate for use in microtransactions, enabling users to trade small amounts of value without the high fees often associated with traditional financial systems.

Beyond the internal economy of the Pi Network, Pi has the potential to be used in a variety of real-world scenarios. As more businesses and merchants begin to recognize the value of cryptocurrencies, Pi could be accepted as a form of payment for a wide range of goods and services. This could include anything from everyday purchases like groceries and clothing to more significant transactions such as travel bookings and digital subscriptions.

The flexibility of Pi, coupled with its ease of use, makes it a promising option for both online and offline commerce.
The types of goods and services that could be exchanged using Pi are vast and varied. In the digital realm, Pi could be used to purchase software, access premium content, or subscribe to online services.

For example, users could pay for cloud storage, streaming services, or e-learning platforms using Pi, benefiting from quick and low-cost transactions. In the physical world, Pi could be used for everything from buying coffee at a local café to paying for a ride-sharing service or even purchasing items from a neighborhood store that accepts cryptocurrency.

Pi's potential as a medium of exchange extends beyond individual transactions. It could also play a role in broader economic activities, such as remittances and cross-border payments. Traditional remittance services often involve high fees and long processing times, particularly for those sending money to family and friends in other countries.

Pi's decentralized nature and mobile-friendly design could offer a more efficient alternative, allowing users to send and receive funds quickly and at a lower cost, regardless of geographic location.
For Pi to realize its full potential as a medium of exchange, integration with existing payment systems and financial institutions is essential.

The ability to convert Pi into fiat currencies or other cryptocurrencies seamlessly will be a critical factor in its adoption. Partnerships with payment processors, banks, and digital wallets could facilitate this integration, making it easier for users to spend their Pi in the broader economy. Additionally, as regulatory frameworks for cryptocurrencies continue to evolve, Pi will need to navigate these landscapes to ensure its acceptance in various jurisdictions.

Another potential use case for Pi is within decentralized finance (DeFi) platforms, where it could be used for lending, borrowing, and staking. As the DeFi ecosystem grows, Pi could become a valuable asset within this space, offering users an alternative to traditional financial services. By participating in DeFi protocols, Pi holders could earn interest, provide liquidity, or engage in other financial activities that are typically reserved for more established cryptocurrencies.

Furthermore, Pi could be used to incentivize participation in the Pi Network's ecosystem. For example, developers could be rewarded in Pi for creating new applications or services that benefit the community. Content creators could earn Pi for their contributions to the network, whether through educational materials, tutorials, or other forms of digital content. This would not only drive engagement within the network but also help to build a vibrant and diverse economy around Pi.

The ability of Pi to integrate with other blockchain networks could also open up new opportunities for its use as a medium of exchange. Interoperability with other cryptocurrencies and decentralized platforms could enable Pi to be used in multi-chain transactions, further expanding its utility.

For instance, Pi could be used as a bridge currency in cross-chain exchanges, facilitating the transfer of value between different blockchain networks. This could position Pi as a key player in the future of decentralized finance, where seamless interactions between different digital assets are increasingly important.

As Pi continues to develop, its role as a medium of exchange will likely evolve in response to the needs and preferences of its user base. Whether used for everyday purchases, cross-border payments, or participation in decentralized finance, Pi has the potential to become a widely accepted and trusted currency in the digital economy.
The key to realizing this potential will be fostering a strong and active community that is committed to building and sustaining the Pi ecosystem.

Key Takeaway: Considering Pi's potential use cases and its success as a medium of exchange will depend not only on the technology behind it but also on the willingness of users and businesses to embrace it.

As more people become familiar with Pi and its benefits, the possibilities for its use will expand, creating new opportunities for economic activity both within and beyond the Pi Network.

(It's important to note that as of the time of writing this book, Pi coin is seen to have been accepted as a medium of exchange in some places and business by its early adopters).

Developing Decentralized Applications(DApps)

Decentralized applications, commonly known as DApps, represent a new wave of software innovation built on blockchain networks. Unlike traditional applications that rely on centralized servers, DApps operate on decentralized networks where no single entity controls the system. This decentralized nature provides greater transparency, security, and resilience against censorship, making DApps an appealing alternative to conventional applications.

They are powered by smart contracts, which are self-executing agreements with the terms of the contract directly written into code. Once deployed on a blockchain, DApps can function autonomously, with the blockchain ensuring that all transactions and interactions are securely recorded and verified without the need for intermediaries.

The potential for developers to create DApps on the Pi Network opens up new possibilities for expanding the network's utility and fostering innovation. Pi's blockchain, designed to be lightweight and mobile-friendly, offers a unique platform for DApp development that is accessible to a broader audience, including those who may not have access to traditional desktop-based blockchain environments.

The Pi Network's mission to democratize cryptocurrency is mirrored in its approach to DApps, where developers from diverse backgrounds and Nations can contribute to the ecosystem by building applications that serve the needs of the community.

One of the most promising areas for DApp development on the Pi Network is decentralized finance, or DeFi. DeFi applications aim to recreate traditional financial services like lending, borrowing, and trading in a decentralized manner, removing the need for banks and other financial intermediaries. On Pi's blockchain, developers could create DApps that allow users to lend their Pi coins to others in exchange for interest, participate in decentralized exchanges, or pool their resources in liquidity pools. The ease of access provided by Pi's mobile-first approach could make DeFi more accessible to individuals who have been traditionally excluded from the financial system, particularly in regions where banking infrastructure is limited.

Another area ripe for DApp development on Pi's blockchain is social media. With concerns about data privacy and control on centralized social platforms, decentralized social media DApps offer an alternative where users have more control over their data and interactions. On the Pi Network, developers could create social media DApps that allow users to share content, communicate, and engage with others in a decentralized environment.

These platforms could operate without the need for centralized servers, reducing the risk of censorship and providing users with the ability to truly own their digital identities.

Additionally, the use of Pi as a native currency within these DApps could enable new forms of monetization, where users are rewarded in Pi for their contributions and interactions on the platform.

Gaming is another field where DApps on the Pi Network could thrive. The intersection of blockchain technology and gaming has given rise to a new genre known as blockchain games, where in-game assets and currencies are represented as tokens on the blockchain.

On Pi's blockchain, developers could create games where players earn Pi coins as they progress, trade in-game assets with other players, or even stake their Pi to participate in tournaments and challenges. The decentralized nature of these games ensures that players have true ownership of their assets, which can be traded or sold outside the game environment. This could lead to a vibrant marketplace within the Pi Network, where digital goods and services are exchanged using Pi as the primary currency.

The potential for DApp development on the Pi Network is not limited to these areas alone. The flexibility of blockchain technology allows developers to explore a wide range of applications, from decentralized marketplaces to identity verification systems.

For example, a DApp could be created to facilitate peer-to-peer transactions within the Pi Network, enabling users to buy and sell goods and services directly using Pi. Another DApp could provide secure, decentralized identity verification, allowing users to prove their identity without relying on centralized authorities. The possibilities are vast, and as the Pi Network grows, so too will the opportunities for developers to innovate and build applications that serve the needs of the global Pi community.

Key Takeaway: Considering the future of DApp development on the Pi Network, the importance is accessibility and inclusivity. By lowering the barriers to entry for both developers and users, Pi's blockchain has the potential to democratize access to decentralized applications, making them available to a much wider audience than ever before.

As more developers begin to build on the Pi Network, we can expect to see a diverse range of DApps that cater to different needs and interests, further enriching the Pi ecosystem and driving its adoption(Note that Pi network as of now already gotten a lot of DApps build on the Pi blockchain, eg, Pi Mall, Pijob. cn, Pitogo, Pibox, etc).

Chapter 7

Believers vs. Skeptics Perspectives on Pi

The Optimistic View and Why Pi Could Succeed

Supporters of the Pi Network often emphasize its innovative approach to cryptocurrency and its potential to democratize access to digital assets. One of the primary arguments in favor of Pi is its unique mobile mining system.

Unlike traditional cryptocurrencies that require significant computational power and energy consumption, Pi allows users to mine coins using their smartphones. This lower barrier to entry makes it easier for individuals across various demographics, including those in developing regions, to participate in the cryptocurrency ecosystem. The mobile-first approach aligns with Pi's mission to make cryptocurrency accessible to a broader audience, which supporters believe could drive widespread adoption.

Another compelling feature of Pi Network is its emphasis on building a strong community. The network's design encourages users to invite friends and family, creating a network effect that can significantly boost its growth potential. By leveraging personal connections, Pi aims to establish a large, engaged user base before fully launching its mainnet.

This community-driven approach is seen as a strategic advantage, helping to build trust and foster engagement among its members. Supporters argue that this grassroots expansion can provide a solid foundation for Pi's long-term success.

Furthermore, the Pi Network's vision includes integration with existing financial systems and services. As the network matures, there is potential for Pi to be used in real-world transactions and partnerships with businesses. For example, if merchants and service providers accept Pi as a form of payment, it could enhance its utility and credibility.

Additionally, collaborations with other blockchain platforms and payment processors could facilitate the exchange of Pi for other cryptocurrencies or fiat currencies, broadening its application and market presence.

Real-world usage examples underscore Pi's potential. In some communities, Pi is already being used for transactions within the network, such as purchasing digital goods or accessing exclusive content. While the mainnet is still under development, early adopters and advocates are experimenting with these use cases, providing valuable insights into how Pi could function in a broader economic context. These preliminary applications demonstrate that Pi has the capacity to integrate into existing systems and offer practical benefits to its users.

A notable aspect of Pi's potential lies in its alignment with emerging trends in decentralized finance and blockchain technology. As the global financial landscape evolves, there is increasing interest in digital currencies and decentralized applications.

Pi's focus on mobile accessibility and community engagement positions it well to capitalize on these trends. By providing a user-friendly platform and fostering an active community, Pi could become a significant player in the evolving digital economy.

In summary, the optimism surrounding Pi Network is driven by its innovative approach to cryptocurrency mining, its community-centric model, and its potential for real-world applications. As the network continues to develop and expand, its unique features and strategic vision could contribute to its overall success in the competitive cryptocurrency landscape.

Key Takeaway: Pi's approach to democratizing access to digital assets and building a strong user base offers a promising foundation for future growth and adoption.

The Critical View, Skepticism, and Concerns

Skeptics of the Pi Network express a range of concerns regarding its long-term viability and overall impact. One major point of criticism revolves around the network's lack of a fully operational mainnet.

Critics argue that without a fully functional blockchain, Pi's value proposition remains theoretical, and its utility is not yet demonstrated in real-world applications. This absence of a live network makes it difficult for skeptics to evaluate Pi's effectiveness or reliability compared to established cryptocurrencies like Bitcoin or Ethereum.

Another significant issue is related to the network's business model and its method of incentivizing participation. Critics question the sustainability of Pi's approach, which relies heavily on building a large user base through mobile mining and referrals. Some argue that this model could be designed more for user acquisition rather than creating real value. Additionally, there are concerns about the potential for users to be misled by the promise of future rewards without a clear mechanism for realizing those rewards. This uncertainty raises questions about whether the network's incentives will translate into genuine value and usability in the future.

Gaining credibility and trust is another challenge for Pi Network. In the cryptocurrency community, established platforms and projects typically build trust through transparency, proven technology, and a track record of successful operations.

Pi's relatively recent entry into the market and its unproven technology make it harder for the network to gain the same level of trust. Furthermore, some critics view Pi's mobile mining approach as a marketing strategy rather than a legitimate technological advancement, which can undermine its credibility.

The potential risks associated with investing time and resources in Pi Network are also a concern. For users who invest significant time in building their Pi holdings, there is a risk that the network may not achieve its stated goals or that it may face insurmountable technical or regulatory hurdles.

The speculative nature of cryptocurrency investments means that even if Pi Network succeeds in launching its mainnet, the value and utility of Pi coins are uncertain. This uncertainty poses a risk for individuals who may invest substantial effort or resources into the network based on the hope of future returns.

In summary, while Pi Network presents an innovative approach to cryptocurrency and aims to democratize access to digital assets, it also faces substantial skepticism and criticism. Concerns about its unproven technology, business model, and credibility contribute to the cautious outlook held by many in the cryptocurrency community.

Key Takeaway: While Pi Network may hold potential, it is crucial for participants to carefully consider these criticisms and the risks before investing significant time or resources.

Chapter 8

Pi Network in the Global Cryptocurrency Landscape

How Pi Compares to Established Cryptocurrencies

The Pi Network presents a unique entry into the global cryptocurrency landscape, and comparing it to established cryptocurrencies such as Bitcoin, Ethereum, Litecoin, Tron, and Solana reveals both its distinct advantages and challenges.

Bitcoin, the pioneering cryptocurrency, is renowned for its robust security and wide acceptance. It operates on a proof-of-work model that, while highly secure, is energy-intensive.

In contrast, Pi Network aims to be more accessible by using mobile mining, a method that is less resource-intensive and designed to be user-friendly, but it has yet to demonstrate the same level of security and decentralization.

Ethereum, known for its smart contract functionality, supports a diverse range of decentralized applications and has played a pivotal role in the development of decentralized finance (DeFi). Pi Network's approach, focusing on mobile accessibility, lacks the sophisticated smart contract capabilities that Ethereum offers, which limits its current application in the broader DeFi space.

However, if Pi Network develops its own robust smart contract capabilities, it could potentially offer new opportunities for developers and users.

Litecoin, often referred to as the silver to Bitcoin's gold, offers faster transaction times and lower fees compared to Bitcoin. Pi

Network, with its mobile-first strategy, seeks to achieve similar goals of accessibility and efficiency, albeit through a different approach. While Litecoin has established itself as a practical alternative to Bitcoin, Pi Network's success in achieving its goals will depend on how effectively it can transition from its current phase to a fully functional and widely accepted cryptocurrency.

Tron and Solana are known for their high throughput and low transaction costs, aiming to address scalability issues seen in other cryptocurrencies. Tron focuses on decentralized content sharing and smart contracts, while Solana emphasizes speed and scalability for decentralized applications.

Pi Network's mobile-centric approach sets it apart but raises questions about its ability to match the scalability and transaction speed of these established networks. As Pi Network evolves, its ability to address scalability concerns will be crucial in determining its long-term viability and success in the competitive market.

The strengths of Pi Network include its emphasis on inclusivity and accessibility through mobile mining, which lowers the entry barrier for new users. This approach has the potential to attract a large, diverse user base.

However, the network's weaknesses include its unproven technology and the challenge of transitioning from a test phase to a fully operational blockchain.
Unlike established cryptocurrencies that have demonstrated their technology and use cases, Pi Network must overcome significant hurdles to gain credibility and achieve its market potential.

Pi Network has the potential to carve out its niche by focusing on its unique selling points, such as mobile accessibility and community-driven growth. If it can successfully address its current limitations and leverage its innovative approach to build a strong, engaged user base, it could establish itself as a distinct player in the cryptocurrency space.

Key Takeaway: While Pi Network offers a novel approach to cryptocurrency, it must go through significant challenges and comparisons with established cryptocurrencies. Its success will depend on how well it can transition from a concept to a widely accepted digital currency, leveraging its strengths while addressing its weaknesses.

The Role of Pi in Developing Economies

Pi Network presents a unique opportunity for developing economies by offering access to digital currency and financial services that are often limited in these regions. In many developing countries, traditional financial infrastructure is sparse, and a significant portion of the population remains unbanked.

Pi Network's mobile-first approach allows individuals to participate in the cryptocurrency space without the need for expensive hardware or extensive technical knowledge. By simply using a smartphone, users can mine Pi coins and engage with a digital financial ecosystem, which could help bridge the gap between the unbanked and financial services.

Financial inclusion is a critical issue in many developing economies, where access to banking and financial services is often restricted by geographic and economic barriers. Pi Network's model of mobile mining and community-driven growth can potentially empower underbanked populations by providing a new avenue for economic participation. The low entry barriers associated with mobile mining make it accessible to a broader audience, including those in remote or underserved areas. This accessibility could encourage greater financial literacy and involvement in the global economy, fostering economic development and individual empowerment.

Real-world adoption of Pi Network in developing regions offers promising insights into its potential impact. In some areas, Pi Network is already gaining traction as individuals and communities begin to explore its possibilities.

For instance, small businesses and local entrepreneurs in these regions are starting to accept Pi as a form of payment, integrating it into their operations to leverage its growing user base. These early adopters are using Pi to facilitate transactions and offer new financial opportunities within their local economies. This grassroots adoption highlights the potential for Pi to contribute to economic activity and financial inclusion in areas that traditionally lack robust financial infrastructure.

Key Takeaway: Pi Network holds significant promise for developing economies by offering accessible digital currency and financial services. Its mobile-first approach and low entry barriers make it a potential game-changer for financial inclusion and economic empowerment in underbanked regions.

As the network grows and more individuals and businesses begin to adopt Pi, it could play a pivotal role in integrating these economies into the global digital financial system.

Chapter 9

The Path to Pi's Mainnet

From Testnet to Mainnet

Pi Network's development journey from its Beta phase to the anticipated Mainnet launch has been marked by careful planning, technological innovation, and community involvement. The Beta phase served as the initial testing ground, allowing users to join the network and begin mining Pi using their smartphones.

During this phase, the network's architecture was designed to be user-friendly and accessible, ensuring that even those with limited technical knowledge could participate. The simplicity of the Beta phase attracted a diverse user base, setting the foundation for Pi's rapid growth.

Following the Beta phase, the Pi Network transitioned to the Testnet phase, a critical step in its development. The Testnet phase is where the network's underlying technology and security protocols are rigorously tested. This phase allows developers to identify and address potential issues in a controlled environment before launching the Mainnet.

For users, the Testnet phase represents a period of anticipation and preparation. It is during this phase that the community can provide feedback, contribute to the network's growth, and prepare for the eventual transition to the Mainnet.

The transition from Testnet to Mainnet is one of the most significant milestones in Pi Network's development. The Mainnet launch is the point at which the network will operate independently of the Testnet environment, becoming a fully functional and decentralized blockchain. For users, this marks the moment when Pi coins can potentially be used in real-world transactions, and the network's value proposition begins to materialize. The Mainnet phase is not just a technical achievement; it represents the culmination of the community's efforts and the realization of Pi's vision as a global cryptocurrency.

To reach the Mainnet, Pi Network must achieve several technical and community milestones. Technically, the network needs to demonstrate its ability to handle large volumes of transactions securely and efficiently. This includes optimizing the consensus algorithm, ensuring the security of the network, and integrating essential features such as smart contracts.

On the community side, building a robust and engaged user base is crucial. The network's success depends on the active participation of its users, who contribute to the security and decentralization of the network through the creation of Security Circles and referrals.

The journey from Beta to Mainnet is also about fostering trust and credibility within the broader cryptocurrency community. Pi Network faces the challenge of proving that it can deliver on its promises of accessibility, security, and decentralization. This involves continuous communication with the community, transparency in development processes, and addressing any concerns or skepticism that may arise. As the network approaches the Mainnet launch, these factors will play a crucial role in determining its acceptance and success in the competitive cryptocurrency landscape.

Key Takeaway: Pi Network's development from Beta to Mainnet is a carefully orchestrated process that requires both technological innovation and community involvement. Each phase is significant, not only for the technical progress it represents but also for the growing sense of anticipation and participation among users. The path to Mainnet is about more than just launching a cryptocurrency; it's about building a sustainable, user-driven network that has the potential to make a meaningful impact on the global financial system.

As Pi Network continues to evolve, its journey from Testnet to Mainnet will be watched closely by both supporters and skeptics, as it strives to fulfill its vision of a decentralized and accessible cryptocurrency for all.

What to Expect When Pi Goes Live

As Pi Network approaches the launch of its Mainnet, anticipation builds around the potential opportunities and challenges that await. The transition from a Testnet to a fully operational Mainnet represents a critical juncture, offering users and developers a range of possibilities while also presenting new hurdles to overcome.

The activation of Pi's Mainnet is expected to unlock various opportunities, particularly in the areas of trading, job creation, and investment. For early adopters and miners, one of the most significant prospects is the ability to trade Pi coins on cryptocurrency exchanges.

This step would enable users to convert their mined Pi into other digital currencies or fiat money, thereby realizing the tangible value of their accumulated assets. Beyond trading, the Mainnet launch could spur the creation of new jobs within the Pi ecosystem. As the network grows, there will likely be increased demand for developers, marketers, legal experts, and other professionals who can contribute to the expansion of the Pi economy.

Additionally, the Mainnet could attract investors seeking to support projects built on Pi's blockchain or to acquire Pi coins as part of a diversified digital asset portfolio. For entrepreneurs and businesses, this transition presents a unique opportunity to create and deploy decentralized applications (DApps) that leverage Pi's user base and blockchain technology, opening up new markets and revenue streams.

However, the transition to Mainnet is not without its challenges. Regulatory issues are a primary concern, as governments around the world continue to develop frameworks for cryptocurrency use and compliance. Pi Network must navigate these evolving regulations to avoid potential legal setbacks that could hinder its growth or limit its accessibility.

Market competition also poses a significant challenge. The cryptocurrency landscape is already crowded, with established players like Bitcoin and Ethereum dominating the space. Pi will need to differentiate itself by offering unique value propositions, such as its focus on accessibility through mobile mining and its large, engaged user community.

Maintaining and enhancing security is another critical concern. As Pi transitions to Mainnet, it will be crucial to protect the network against potential cyber threats, ensuring the integrity and trustworthiness of the blockchain. Scaling the network to handle increased transaction volumes without compromising performance or security will also be a key focus.

As the Mainnet launch draws near, users and developers alike can take proactive steps to prepare for this new phase. For users, securing their Pi accounts with robust authentication methods is essential to protect their assets as the network expands. Staying informed about the latest developments and understanding the potential impacts of the Mainnet on their Pi holdings will enable users to make informed decisions.

For developers, now is the time to explore the possibilities of building on Pi's blockchain. By familiarizing themselves with the network's technical specifications and tools, developers can position themselves to capitalize on the demand for new DApps and services within the Pi ecosystem.
Engaging with the Pi community and contributing to discussions about the network's future can also help developers gain insights and build connections that will be valuable as the ecosystem grows.

Key Takeaway: The Mainnet launch represents both an exciting opportunity and a significant challenge for Pi Network. The potential for trading, job creation, and investment is substantial, but the network must also navigate regulatory hurdles, market competition, and security concerns.

By preparing for these challenges and seizing the opportunities that arise, users and developers can play a crucial role in shaping the future of Pi Network as it transitions to Mainnet and beyond. The success of Pi will depend not only on its technological advancements but also on the active participation and collaboration of its global community.

Chapter 10

The Future of Pi and Cryptocurrency

Predicting Pi's Impact on the Global Economy

The rise of Pi Network represents a new chapter in the evolution of cryptocurrency and its potential to reshape the global economy. As digital finance continues to gain momentum, Pi's unique approach could position it as a significant force in this transformation, particularly in the realms of decentralized economies and underserved regions.

This analysis will explore Pi's potential long-term impact, how it may influence key trends in cryptocurrency, and speculative

143

insights into its evolution over the next decade.

Pi Network, with its emphasis on accessibility and mobile mining, has the potential to play a transformative role in digital finance.

By making cryptocurrency mining possible through smartphones, Pi is democratizing access to digital currency, allowing people from all walks of life, including those in developing countries, to participate in the global economy. This could have profound implications for financial inclusion, particularly in regions where traditional banking services are limited or nonexistent.

As Pi Network continues to grow, it may contribute to the development of decentralized economies, where individuals and communities can trade and transact directly with each other, bypassing traditional financial intermediaries.

The impact of Pi on the global economy could extend beyond individual users to influence broader trends in cryptocurrency adoption, regulation, and financial innovation. As Pi gains traction, it could drive greater adoption of digital currencies, particularly among populations that have been hesitant to embrace more complex or resource-intensive cryptocurrencies like Bitcoin.

Pi's focus on mobile mining and ease of use could lower the barriers to entry, making cryptocurrency more accessible to a wider audience. This increased adoption could, in turn, prompt governments and regulatory bodies to develop more comprehensive frameworks for digital currencies, potentially leading to greater legitimacy and stability in the market.

Speculating on how Pi might evolve in the next 5-10 years provides a glimpse into its potential trajectory and the broader impact it could have on the global economy.

Here are ten possible developments:

1. **Integration with Financial Institutions**:
As Pi matures, it could be integrated into existing financial institutions as a digital currency option for transactions, savings, and investments. This could lead to partnerships with banks, fintech companies, and payment processors, further embedding Pi into the global financial system.

2. **Expansion of Decentralized Applications (DApps)**:
Pi's blockchain could become a hub for decentralized applications, enabling a wide range of services, from peer-to-peer lending and insurance to decentralized social networks and gaming platforms. This expansion could drive innovation and attract developers to build on the Pi Network.

3. **Growth in E-Commerce and Online Marketplaces**:
Pi could be widely adopted as a payment method in e-commerce platforms and online

marketplaces, offering an alternative to traditional payment systems like credit cards and PayPal. This could enhance the speed, security, and cost-effectiveness of online transactions.

4. Empowerment of Underserved Communities:
In regions with limited access to traditional banking, Pi could become a critical tool for economic empowerment, enabling people to save, invest, and transact in ways that were previously unavailable to them. This could lead to increased economic activity and growth in these areas.

5. Influence on Cryptocurrency Regulation:
As Pi gains popularity, it could play a role in shaping cryptocurrency regulations. Governments may look to Pi as a model for how digital currencies can be made accessible and secure, influencing the development of regulatory frameworks that

support innovation while protecting consumers.

6. Adoption in Remittance Markets:
Pi could become a preferred currency for remittances, particularly in regions where traditional remittance services are expensive or difficult to access. By enabling low-cost, cross-border transactions, Pi could reduce the cost of sending money to family members abroad and increase the efficiency of the remittance market.

7. Integration with Internet of Things (IoT):
As the Internet of Things continues to grow, Pi could be integrated into IoT devices, enabling secure and automated transactions between connected devices. This could lead to new use cases for Pi in areas such as smart cities, autonomous vehicles, and home automation.

8. Role in Digital Identity Management:

Pi's blockchain could be used to create secure, decentralized digital identities, enabling users to verify their identity online without relying on centralized authorities. This could have applications in areas such as voting, access to government services, and online security.

9. Expansion into Tokenized Assets:
Pi could evolve into a platform for tokenizing real-world assets, such as real estate, art, and commodities. This would enable users to trade fractional ownership of these assets on the Pi blockchain, potentially opening up new investment opportunities for a broader audience.

10. Evolution of Governance Models:
As Pi grows, it could experiment with new forms of decentralized governance, allowing users to have a say in the network's development and decision-making processes. This could lead to more democratic and transparent management of

the Pi Network, setting a precedent for other cryptocurrencies to follow.

In summary, the future of Pi Network holds immense promise, both for its users and the broader global economy. By making cryptocurrency more accessible and fostering the development of decentralized economies, Pi has the potential to drive significant change in digital finance and financial inclusion. As it evolves, Pi could influence trends in cryptocurrency adoption, regulation, and innovation, helping to shape the future of the digital economy.

Key Takeaway: While the path ahead is uncertain, the possibilities for Pi are vast, and its impact on the global economy could be profound. Whether it succeeds in achieving these ambitions will depend on the collective efforts of its community, developers, and supporters, as well as its ability to adapt to the challenges and opportunities that lie ahead.

What Comes After Pi?

As the cryptocurrency landscape continues to evolve, Pi Network's emergence is a pivotal moment that signals the broader trajectory of digital currencies and blockchain technology. While Pi has already made waves by introducing a more accessible form of cryptocurrency through mobile mining, it raises an essential question: What lies beyond Pi?

The future of cryptocurrency and blockchain technology holds tremendous potential, with new trends and innovations poised to redefine what digital currencies can achieve.

Cryptocurrency has already transformed the financial world, but the journey is far from over. The digital currency ecosystem will continue to grow, driven by an ongoing quest for greater efficiency, scalability, and inclusivity. One key area of focus will be enhancing the interoperability of various blockchain networks.

As more cryptocurrencies and blockchain applications emerge, the ability for these networks to communicate and operate seamlessly with one another will become increasingly important. This could lead to the development of more sophisticated protocols that enable different blockchains to interact, creating a more unified and efficient ecosystem.

Decentralized finance (DeFi) has already shown its potential to disrupt traditional financial systems, but its future holds even more transformative possibilities. The rise of DeFi marks a shift towards a more decentralized and user-controlled financial landscape, where individuals can access a wide range of financial services without relying on intermediaries.

As this sector matures, we can expect the creation of increasingly complex financial instruments and services that leverage blockchain's transparency and security. Pi Network, with its large and engaged user base, could play a significant role in the ongoing development of DeFi, providing a platform for new and innovative decentralized applications.

Privacy and security will remain at the forefront of cryptocurrency development. As blockchain technology evolves, there will be a growing emphasis on enhancing privacy features to protect users' identities and transactions. Emerging technologies like zero-knowledge proofs and homomorphic encryption offer promising solutions that could be integrated into future cryptocurrencies.

These advancements will ensure that users can engage in transactions with complete privacy, without compromising the transparency and trust that are fundamental to blockchain technology.
The environmental impact of cryptocurrency mining has been a significant concern, particularly with energy-intensive proof-of-work (PoW) systems. Moving

forward, we can anticipate a shift towards more energy-efficient consensus mechanisms. Pi Network's mobile-friendly, energy-efficient approach is a step in this direction, but future cryptocurrencies may adopt even more sustainable practices, such as proof-of-stake (PoS) or other innovative protocols that minimize environmental impact. As global awareness of climate change grows, the demand for greener cryptocurrencies will likely increase, driving further innovation in this area.

Another trend that will shape the future of cryptocurrency is the tokenization of real-world assets. Blockchain technology enables the creation of digital tokens that represent ownership of physical assets, such as real estate, art, or commodities. This could revolutionize the way assets are bought, sold, and traded, making it easier for individuals to invest in fractional ownership and diversify their portfolios.

Pi Network could potentially expand into this space, offering its users new opportunities to participate in the tokenized economy.

The integration of artificial intelligence (AI) with blockchain technology is another exciting frontier. AI has the potential to enhance the security, efficiency, and scalability of blockchain networks by optimizing processes, predicting market trends, and automating complex tasks.

The combination of AI and blockchain could lead to the development of smarter, more autonomous digital currencies that can adapt to changing market conditions in real-time. Pi Network, with its forward-thinking approach, could be at the forefront of this integration, driving the next wave of innovation in the cryptocurrency space.

As blockchain technology becomes more advanced, we may see the rise of decentralized autonomous organizations

(DAOs) as a dominant force in the digital economy. DAOs are organizations that operate entirely on blockchain networks, governed by smart contracts rather than centralized entities. They allow for a more democratic and transparent decision-making process, where all stakeholders have a voice.

The future could see DAOs managing everything from investment funds to social networks, with Pi Network potentially playing a key role in facilitating these new forms of organization.

The evolution of quantum computing presents both challenges and opportunities for cryptocurrency. Quantum computers have the potential to break the cryptographic algorithms that currently secure blockchain networks, posing a significant threat to the entire cryptocurrency ecosystem.

However, the development of quantum-resistant algorithms could safeguard digital currencies against these threats. As this technology advances, Pi

Network and other cryptocurrencies will need to adapt to maintain their security and integrity in the face of quantum computing.

The future of cryptocurrency will also be shaped by regulatory developments. As governments and financial institutions recognize the growing influence of digital currencies, they are likely to implement more comprehensive regulatory frameworks. These regulations could provide much-needed clarity and legitimacy to the cryptocurrency market, encouraging broader adoption.

However, they could also introduce new challenges, such as compliance requirements and restrictions on certain activities. Pi Network will need to navigate these regulatory landscapes carefully, balancing innovation with adherence to legal standards.

Finally, the social impact of cryptocurrency should not be underestimated. As digital currencies become more mainstream, they have the potential to reshape the way people interact with money and each other. Cryptocurrencies could empower individuals in developing regions, providing them with access to financial services that were previously out of reach. They could also foster new forms of community and collaboration, as people come together to build and support decentralized networks. Pi Network, with its global user base and inclusive approach, is well-positioned to lead this social transformation.

In summary, the future of cryptocurrency and blockchain technology is full of possibilities, and Pi Network could play a pivotal role in this evolution. From the integration of AI and quantum computing to the rise of DAOs and tokenized assets, the next generation of digital currencies will be shaped by a wide range of emerging trends and technologies.

As Pi Network continues to grow and adapt, it has the potential to not only influence these developments but also to redefine what is possible in the world of digital finance.

Key Takeaway: While the future is uncertain, the opportunities for innovation and impact in the cryptocurrency space are vast, and Pi Network is uniquely positioned to be at the forefront of this exciting journey.

Pi Network White Paper

Scan This QR Code To Access The White Paper

Scan Me

CONCLUSION

As we arrive at this point, it's clear that PiCoin, Pi Network, and its innovative blockchain technology are more than just a fleeting experiment—they are a bold step toward a more inclusive and accessible digital economy. From the initial vision to the intricate mechanisms that power the network, Pi represents a new frontier in cryptocurrency, one that is designed for everyone, everywhere.

The journey from concept to reality has been marked by ingenuity, resilience, and a steadfast commitment to empowering individuals across the globe. Pi Network has the potential to redefine the way we interact with digital currency, offering unprecedented opportunities for financial inclusion and innovation.

As we look to the future, Pi's success will hinge on the continued dedication of its community, the evolution of its technology, and its ability to navigate the complexities of the global financial landscape. The chapters we've explored together serve as both a foundation and a roadmap for what lies ahead.

The story of Pi is far from over—it's just beginning.

ENCOURAGEMENT

As the author of this exploration into PiCoin, Pi Network, and its groundbreaking blockchain technology, I want to take a moment to speak directly to you, the reader. If you've made it this far, you've journeyed through the intricacies of a network that is not just another addition to the vast cryptocurrency landscape but a beacon of potential. The future holds tremendous promise, and I hope you're as excited as I am about what lies ahead.

Imagine a world where financial systems are no longer the exclusive domain of the elite, where the underbanked and unbanked have the same opportunities as those in the wealthiest corners of the globe.

Pi Network is not merely a concept; it's a catalyst for change, a force that could very well reshape how we think about value, currency, and community.

But let's not pretend the road ahead will be smooth. Like any groundbreaking innovation, Pi will face its share of skeptics, hurdles, and unexpected twists. There will be moments when progress seems slow, where doubts may creep in—both within the community and in your own mind.

These challenges are not obstacles; they serve as stepping stones. Each twist in the story of Pi Network only adds to its richness, making the eventual success all the more rewarding.

Think of Pi Network as a novel with multiple layers—each layer revealing more depth, more intrigue, and more potential than the last. You, as a member of this growing community, are not just a passive reader; you are a co-author of this story. Every interaction you have, every Pi you mine, every conversation you spark about this network contributes to a narrative that could redefine digital currency and decentralized economies.

Consider the twists we've seen so far—the shift from skepticism to cautious optimism, the gradual build-up of a secure and scalable network, the emergence of Pi as a medium of exchange in developing economies. Each of these developments has been a plot point in the story of Pi, each one drawing us closer to a future where Pi isn't just a possibility but a reality.

As we move forward, I encourage you to keep an open mind and an optimistic heart. The success of Pi Network is not just in the technology but in the community—people like you who believe in the potential for a more inclusive, decentralized financial world. The uncertainty of the future is what makes it so exciting. The next chapter of Pi's story is unwritten, and it's up to all of us to pen it.

So, stay engaged, stay hopeful, and most importantly, stay curious. The twists and turns will come, but they will only make the final destination more meaningful. Together, we can ensure that Pi Network doesn't just become another footnote in the annals of cryptocurrency but a defining chapter in the story of global financial evolution.

The best is yet to come, and with your participation, it will be extraordinary.

Dear Readers,

Your journey through this Pi guidebook is just the beginning of something extraordinary. If you've found value in these pages, I invite you to share your positive thoughts and experiences. Genuine reviews not only help others discover this guide, but they also strengthen our shared commitment to exploring the future of Pi Network and cryptocurrency.

Whether you purchased this book online or received it as a gift, your feedback is invaluable. Please take a moment to leave a review where you got this book, and don't hesitate to share your insights on your social media platforms. Your voice can inspire others to join the Pi community and explore the limitless possibilities it offers.

Thank you for joining us on this journey.
Your support means everything.

NOTE

NOTE

NOTE

www.ingramcontent.com/pod-product-compliance
Lightning Source LLC
Chambersburg PA
CBHW031630210526
45464CB00004B/1831